The Arsonist's Letters

The Arsonist's Letters Michael Tyrell

A pioneering publishing house dedicated to creating intelligent, vivid books. Established to inform, educate, entertain and provoke.

A Backlash Press Book

First published 2021
Reprinted 2024

backlashpress.com

Book designer: The Scrutineer, Rachael Adams.

Printed and bound by IngramSpark

ISBN: 978-0-9956843-4-8

All rights reserved. No part of this publication may be reproduced, stored in a retrieval system or transmitted in any form or by any means, electronic, mechanical, photocopying, recording or otherwise, without permission of the copyright holder.

Copyright © Michael Tyrell
The moral rights of the author have been asserted.

Michael Tyrell

The Arsonist's Letters Michael Tyrell

Backlash Poetry

American Dangerous: Renée Olander
Bombing the Thinker: Darren C. Demaree
Clay Unbreakables: Natalia I. Andrievskikh
Into The The: Robin Reagler
Phantom Laundry: Michael Tyrell
Tattered Scrolls and Postulates: Joseph V. Milford
The Life in the Sky Comes Down: Bruce Bromley
Unfinished Murder Ballads: Darren C. Demaree

Backlash Journals

#1
#2
#3: Provoke
#4
Isolation
#5

The Arsonist's Letters Michael Tyrell

Cover collage by Michael Tyrell
Author portrait artwork by Richard Castro

Contents

The Invitations
Birthday, Anniversary, Sympathy, Blank　　15
The Primal Scene　　17
Cult　　19

The Garden
Alphabet City, 1994　　25
The Garden　　27
Glass Zodiac, 1996　　29
Landscape with a Burning City　　31

Letters Written Near the End of the Cold War
Nixon　　35
Custody　　37
Intruder　　39
Of Hospices and Hopscotch　　41
Letters Written Near the End of the Cold War　　45

All Saints' Day
Transit　　51
Delicatessen　　53

Fayum
All the Unreal Animals　　61
Alice, Sweet Alice　　63
The Passwords　　65
Letter Sent Back Through Time to Mussolini's Italy　　67

Wearable Ammunition
Hemingway　　73
Wormhole　　75

Lontano	77
Murder in Sea Gate	79
Wound Care	81

The Ones With Children

Letter at the Security Gate	85
In Clinton Hill, After Seeing the House Where the Famous Poet Lived Until the Area Became "Unsafe"	87
In Winter the Only Green	89
At Salvation	91
Marathon	93
Documentary for Eleanor Marzano, Who Was Mistaken for the Kidnapped Lindbergh Baby in March, 1932	95
Two Postcards	97
To Have Them	99
Apology to the Letters	101
Notes	105
Acknowledgements	107
A Note about The Author	109

The Arsonist's Letters
Michael Tyrell

The Arsonist's Letters Michael Tyrell

> My own friends, not written back,
> not called. Oh our love
> turned from, and August half over.
> —Jean Valentine, *"The Summer Was Not Long Enough"*

> The past
> will shed some light, but never keep us warm.
> —Daniel Hall, *"Love-Letter-Burning"*

The Arsonist's Letters Michael Tyrell

The Invitations

The Arsonist's Letters Michael Tyrell

Birthday Anniversary Sympathy Blank

She thought of zoos in parks, how when cities were under siege, during world wars, people ate the animals.
—Lorrie Moore, *"You're Ugly, Too"*

I go to market to buy every card I can think of
but they are out. The racks are empty & I can't help
picturing a vacant zoo because the animals are eaten
because there's a war on, & why people say
abattoir when they really mean *slaughterhouse*.
The clerk informs me, "We are not making cards anymore.
From now on it will be only singing microchips
and hologram cakes, a sexy dream downloaded
into the brain the evening before a big day."
My order would be too late, anyway. It is your birthday
and they have you in Intensive Care, in the unit
a semiprivate. You think that sounds military & erotic.
Are you sure there are no cards left? "I'll check," the clerk says,
pickle-faced, slithering down his corridor of monitors.
A woman on one console goes on & on about satellites,
how every satellite has a pulse, & itinerants from other planets,
if they have hearts, will know what we are, what substance
is beating or brooking or conspiring against us.
Birthday, Anniversary, Sympathy, Blank.
I can't ever pretend to browse but I somehow like the wall murals,
the idealized George Eliot & her self-possessed smirk,
I can't remember a word from her novels,
have I finished any of them, here I am somewhere
between *Adam Bede* & *Daniel Deronda*,
and it's your birthday & Intensive Care has you,
you are expiring & by now you are expired, I'll have to
redirect the subscription & collect the insurance,
delete you from my database, laser out the tattoo,
scribble the obit, hock the potboilers with your name in them,

The Arsonist's Letters Michael Tyrell

white-out the embarrassing marginalia,
suck dry the account, dishonor the ticket, unearth the certificate,
permanently pull the phone like a bad tooth,
chip down the initialed box elder, edit all anecdotes
to the past tense, chuck the leftover tangelos,
let the koi back into the pond, dump your cacti,
scissor your documents because the shredder's broken,
let your memoirs fall into the bathwater so no one can read them,
think up replies to insults I could never answer,
donate your gabardines, find significance in our ultimate
exchanges, appease your creditors, & saw the futon in half.
There's always the risk of an invitation finding its way to you,
not unlike the poor dead coffee heiress who got one decades later.
The naked guy sprints around the store,
a rabid mongrel loose in a Vatican.
Those who make us secure will arrive before my clerk.
If someone naked were arrested now would you laugh,
I'm not sure you would stick around for it to happen,
you never cared for surprises, & it's
true, surprise parties were never a surprise to you,
you preferred saying *I was invited* instead of *alive*

The Primal Scene

It's winter, I'm deep in the factory called mother,
near the hum of the conveyor belts—
on one track, things on their way to the boxes,
on another, to the compactor—
before Labyrinth and Thread,
before The Scalpel and The Carnage—

the constant lights-out barracks
and the weeks of scummy assemblage,
the sizzle and grit of world-sounds coming in from the one-way radio.

Time-traveler, stowaway: not accounted for in the temporal world,
nine months not counted toward my earth-time—
body inside body, Russian doll;
one object in several places, an insult to physics.

There are armies outside the walls.
It's an earth you hear them making, a slash-and-burn operation.
Everyone has to be melted down.
They're the trees that must be set on fire,
they're the scorched dirt, a grave
that can store people and the possessive case—

And this is how they do it—this is how to put on a face,
this is how to take it down, this is how
to burn the tree of the body
to make the flower of the face.

The Arsonist's Letters Michael Tyrell

Cult

1 I think my brother has maybe joined a cult.
There must be some reason.
He has cut off everyone.
Or my sense of his everyone.
From his life.
Cuttings.
They, we
won't grow.

2 His wife and daughter,
and my mother and his mother
(dreams reveal them accurately
as two separates who share a body)
each of us separable,
I mean pared and separate,
unpaired. Cards cut,
no scattered, left willy-nilly
playing cards
in a kitchen drawer
after he vanished
from Hackensack—
he said
he was being followed,
he said he paid to follow me—

3 I was the one
always telling creation myths.
Often only to myself.
A frown too thin, a spider too big
to kill I was.

4 Every night a story about beginnings.
One night, I'm ten, he says look up.

The Arsonist's Letters Michael Tyrell

    So? I say.
    Spiders. You can't see them.
    Everything they catch became stars.

5   I cling to the giant's shins.
    First a giant, then a stump,
    almost like the old giving tree martyr,
    then finally an idol.
    Steal it, make it disappear.
    Smash it.
    No, I'll cop to it—
    I didn't know you could
    make yourself a missing person.

6   Twenty years
    after I am twenty.
    Today.
    An email.
    I mean, he answers mine.
    His asthma bothers
    him in Florida; this is the
    clue I know it's him,
    man of no seasons, but
    more troublingly man of no questions,
    says he is
    glad to hear from me—

7   No, I think this is the cult's ruse:
    they've forbidden him everyone past
    but they allow him to communicate
    without making plans, to not arouse
    too much suspicion…

8   His old yearbook, his diploma,
    origin story, all given away.
    To his daughter.
    She sickens, seems to heal,
    plans to marry. The
    mothers in the story
    just seem to sicken.

His email
the woman
from the country of exiles,
from twenty years ago.

9   Is it all creation myth
to the one who flees?
Every morning
tabula rasa. No, it is
Florida, Tampa,
hell for asthma, maybe
the clue an SOS—
I should go help him.
My brother who tried to explain
to our mother what a black hole's
singularity was,
what death meant for a red giant.

10 Tonight, walking through the park,
I went into those spider lines
the trees send down
this time of winter-spring.
They caught me; I looked up.
Drones, maybe the planet Venus.
His ruler. And these
spider threads beautiful
as if you're supposed to overlook
how they bind you.
Just lightly, just for a moment.
This is how they get you.

11 In the same time zone
two of us. Daylight savings.
I bet
he has more stars.
What are the others like.

The Arsonist's Letters Michael Tyrell

The Garden

The Arsonist's Letters Michael Tyrell

Alphabet City, 1994

        To the loft and to them I came
to be the opiate, not the administered,
        fiending to become the body
without self, reversible as a jacket, Able Was
        I Ere I Saw Elba, as the *trompe
l'oeil* in Psych remaining two faces
        human, the Queen and her
Consort, seen from another angle
        as invaluable vase, change the
room of the high and the heart
        recognizes, stops, the sober
keeps moving, show-
        ing me snapshots, waterfall
and the others on
        the floor, I fall backward
into that morning, I
        pass a butcher shop, apron
a slick watchman, I
        carry a tied package leaking
through brown paper, red-
        handed I learn to walk
and deceive what I
        love, I love the blindered
light bandaging the
        motionless, construction
24-7, like the home of the Winchester
        widow, corridors lead-
ing to sealed walls, stairways
        done in mid-air to
beguile phantoms, I come to a corner
        & I hear myself outside the door

The Arsonist's Letters Michael Tyrell

The Garden

The tuxed-up drunk, trembling the dorm's lobby window
when a bottle tipped him over. His squint not at me but past me
to the one hundred keys glittering behind my post,

the check-in desk, where all summer, I worked the Saturday
insomnia shift. The ruse of looking down at the marble notebook,
one-one thousand, then looking up: the drunk gone, like a movie ghost.

The prank caller, the phone a bee-sting sound.
The paper I had to write to undo my grade of "Incomplete,"
something about Eden, something to please my professor.

Tumbling from the nightclub: the samba amateurs,
some still whistling and writhing. Cigarettes cracking balloons.
Like archangels, the narcs patrolling closed Union Square.

Kamikaze, Titanic, Banshee: all the sweet nicknames I knew for heroin.
Saying them, obeying them, to feel the lull. To not feel.
The dancers whose other moves frightened me

nights I worked sober: they trashed themselves;
the place, the park, could be the garden again only if
they vanished. This much I knew about Eden.

And that I wasn't safe: I needed to look outside.
The desk radio refreshed deaths and sped-read
the conditions—traffic and weather—

no obit could overrule.
Early morning the beautiful victim, noon the coroner.
The dancers writhed.

The Arsonist's Letters Michael Tyrell

Glass Zodiac, 1996

There's a reason the astronomy prof said
we don't as we don't remember our birth
remember the first eye we look into
or else it remembers us all

Remember he went on Galileo's tragedies
they will be on your final
disbelief failure punishment
disgrace naming names almost turning the *self* in

but what do we know
disbelievers yawning in stadium seats
on my desk planet acronyms
(Mary's virginity ended memorably
joyfully she unbuckled nine passerby)

we want out like the guy
in the learn'd astronomer poem
the outside sky full of its urban blight
broken-bottle glass and broken windows theories
and the zodiac imaginary or too ingenious

not to break like glass animals
wanting out so we can go back in
the gun in the parlor we pay for it to send
bolts through our tongues
so it will teach us a new language
make frescoes on us
nothing to do with armor nor carnage

but class isn't over yet
Pluto still the ninth and last
but not for long he said a fake planet

The Arsonist's Letters Michael Tyrell

then a painted fake of the planet a slide
he beams on the screen

followed by a photo of a human eye
planetary monstrous
a reason we don't remember
he said or else it remembers us all

Landscape With a Burning City

(Pieter Schoubroeck, 1570–1607; oil on canvas)

Who are we, where are we going—I asked the oracle
Once in a dream—why are we sent here blue-faced, half-drowned,
Bald & blind, without armor or language—

Why do every hour almost all of us forget
To ask for another hour—why only just another apple, please—
Why some more milk, just a drop, like orphans—

How did the makers of twins not build them alike—
Whose diamond-eyed boy was it, who ended up on the poster—
When did he—when do the missing *know* they're missing—

What date will the nuclear reactor open, I asked—
It's always about to open—when the nuclear winter—
Where the return of American hostages, how the bullet in the president—

When the oracle opened her mouth—gleaming
Bracelet of teeth, all gold—showed me she had no tongue—& my eyes
Opened—that's when it was the future—places instead of questions—

Wintersummer—leaves rising back into their branches—
& when the skyscrapers turn into torches and collapse—
I am under the skylight at my office, under the roof-top, under the sky—

How—when I am only this body—made to be touched & charred—
How can any picture tell me what it is they see—
The ones on the roof who say *holy fuck, holy fuck, holy fuck—*

The Arsonist's Letters Michael Tyrell

Letters Written Near the End of the Cold War

The Arsonist's Letters Michael Tyrell

Nixon

I was born the summer of his disgrace.
That's always been my claim. And it's a trait
I despise in other people: hitching the intensely personal

to the historical, making Watergate a lame pun for
passage and delivery. But my mother
insists on scandal. An unmarried mother, middle-aged—
she swears her pregnancy didn't show, even
that morning she locked herself in the toilet
and told her own mother to call an ambulance.

The phones rang off the hook that day—
everyone in the family.

If I wanted to carry this further, I could point out
my mother, like Nixon, could've resigned.
A childless cousin wanted to raise me, a maternal
version of a vice-president. But my mother,
a child of Roosevelt, kept me: four terms of depression

and world war. Like all children, I demanded a
recount, a new election: request denied.
Hostage faces bubbled on the television screen.

When she told me who my father was, I wanted
the mystery back—the speculation traded like
missiles between the family gossips, not a Woodward
or Bernstein among them, Deepthroat a man
on the street they couldn't identify, who
never spoke to them.

The Arsonist's Letters Michael Tyrell

Custody

My mother's old now;
she's almost my baby.
Soon she'll have to go to school.

Death will have to take her.
He has her during the week,
I get her on weekends.

I'm like my mother—
neither of us can drive.
The court didn't care for that.
That's why I didn't win full custody.

So, on weekends, my mother and I wait at a bus shelter.
Death's around here someplace—
no such thing as unsupervised visits, with him.

I'd kill for a restraining order,
but that would require his assistance.

I'd accuse him of breaking the bus-shelter window,
but that's not his style. Besides, it's not even real glass,
the way today is spring in writing only,
endorsed by a calendar's soon-to-be-crossed-out square.

Our divorce was amicable;
he wasn't a bad provider,
and everyone says
reconciliation is inevitable.

In fact, he still has his good points.
He lets the bus complete its route,
he lets the market exist.

The Arsonist's Letters Michael Tyrell

With expiration dates
he signs the shelved milk and pills, the batteries
for disaster flashlights—

One turn down the wrong aisle
and I'm the child again,
scanning the market
for my lost mother—

Strangers all I can turn to,
and one I must marry.

Intruder

Behind the blood-pressure bracelets
and their dangling black balloons, among
the gold circle coils of Trojans
waiting for consensus,
near the boxes of moon-dust gloves and sharps
but beyond the examining table's paper sheets
crinkling forward like newsprint etched with
the body's unreadables,
and close enough to the doctor who needs
the snake and silver spool to hear the inaudible heart—
      the cricket caught somewhere inside, hidden.
More rasp than song. More song than siren.
Near the photograph
of the lungs like wilderness for sale
and the vent through which they say, make a fist,
this won't hurt a bit,
and the page on the waiting bench that begins
Of This Self-Planet
that Speaks Most Candidly in Earthquakes and Whispers,
I Will Always Feel Like an Intruder,
like a letter just started, a living will,
and the plasma silvering the funnels
to be tubed and set out all night
in the tin drugless bin
compact as a pet coffin, bright as a mailbox
from a century of letters.

The Arsonist's Letters Michael Tyrell

Of Hospices and Hopscotch

The rock carried from a country she's never been to,
and the rood, and the pill, and the rage,
everyone's cheating her,
and this is the wrong food,
and I'm the messenger,
and so she shoots me.

Take out the blame:
I don't mind, it's the messenger's
obligation, like a dutiful son
hauling out the trash,
though he can never been clean,
having been in the world, probably he's been
shot like me, the stairs the color
of the entry wound,
the neighbors I pass in the hallway
who can't tell if this is just another movie
being shot in the neighborhood.

I'm only sorry the sniper
never got to hear my story
about the girl I saw on my way in
who fell and split her knee.
She would've loved it,
the accidents of children
her favorite parts of secular life—

and it's a shame how my stumbles
rub, smudge off chalk put to concrete.
Hopscotch. The war out here, the grids,
the laws, the ambulances,
and the messengers,
mauve and dusk bullets in hand,

The Arsonist's Letters Michael Tyrell

crumbling out lines, almost roads,
among blood's imperfect circles.

Bottle Episode

A TV episode that usually focuses on one or two characters, on a limited budget, in a small, easily managed set designed for quick shooting.

Time for closeups: the mother and son,
who has said something to her unforgivable,
who has wished him unborn—

so why shouldn't it be like one of those mid-season installments
late in the life of the series itself?
Money and earth in the ruined world, two desperadoes

not unlike Heisenberg and Pinkman
so engaged in their enterprise and requited hate
they have little use for words.

Only a skeleton crew now, a cast of
two. A shared room, INTERIOR TWO NORTH.
Saint Nowhere, -Never, say

the surrounding characters written out.
Who wanted too much money to stay.
Who needed to be killed off. For realism

an aide entering the theater.
Never a doctor. As if, in any reality,
the doctors knew how to conceal themselves.

But Dolores behind the curtain,
waking, Dolores with her word for honey,
the word for nothing.
Saying no, no--is that the one hardest to shake?

Saying no: your story alone isn't worth seeing.

The Arsonist's Letters Michael Tyrell

In the poem you didn't read
(Whatever images I have now, I hoard them.
What words I hold, they conjure and shatter.)

It's the earthly light that never seems to enter the room.
It's the money the show is saving, never leaving the set.
Time for one take, mark it, roll sound, though
you'll have no cliffhanger, hiatus.

No, honey,   nada honey,
Honey   nada,
honey no, bottling the never honey.

Letters Written Near the End of the Cold War

I wonder if you've seen them on the hospital TV—
children on talk shows
who swear live inside them
the entire populations of small countries.

*

Multiples, abreactions—
big, formless hands make multiples, *it's like they
smash an aquarium tank and take all the glass,
then make something that walks and talks like a human being*—
it's the story they don't show you

not only in Edgewise or Northwest Oaks or Rattlewood
or whatever euphemism they you have you in now,
it's the story they won't show you anywhere.

*

I haven't read Rushdie, just know he's in hiding.
Your in hiding's a low security ward,
initials in permanent marker on the tag-ends of shirts.

Still in the world of names—
Swiss Army, Bic, Shelter Island, Poospatuck—

I'm on the late bus whose seats'
cigarette lighter marks and knife-slits
get sealed with What's the Use tape,
the burn-out bus, so you called it,
the bus that still loops by the Poospatuck beach houses—
hilarious, sad, neutral—*the same-worldness of it*—
occult graffiti on Chapter 11 plywood.

The Arsonist's Letters Michael Tyrell

The library won't carry the Rushdie, it carries nothing
but John Updike and Anne Tyler—
They used to have the Satanic Bible
but they had to take that one out.
They used to have a book that—

*

Oh, whatever, fuck it all, you said,
swallowing your one hundred aspirin.

*

Years of school we lived together
where substitute teachers borrowed the names of birds—
years of Mallard, Dove, Pigeon—

remember how you said,
giving everything a name,
that's how Adam fucked it all up....

*

Houses with boats in the yards,
then nothing, then houses
almost prosperous, not yours, not mine,
just me and the driver on the late bus.

*

I count what's absent, a ghost list—

No you who speaks in double negatives,
no you who says I don't not love you.

One blue this way, they said,
one blue that way—

Needs Another Seven Astronauts, they said.

The bad jokes came up like mushrooms after the Challenger burned;

now East is West, West is East in Berlin;
Checkpoint Charlie buys the farm—

It's the names
that fall and don't fall, I see that now,

and M., I don't half-miss you.
Get yourself home.

Our names are deep in the book
and the story makes little sense
but at least you can count on
it always starting with the same naked man
making the same indelible mistakes.

The Arsonist's Letters Michael Tyrell

All Saints' Day

The Arsonist's Letters Michael Tyrell

Transit

Inside the shelter of another morning.
The escaping minutes that bottle bees ride,
phone numbers carved into the walls.
The three battered walls where they wait.
Where I wait, inside another morning.
Inside another morning and no fourth wall.
Tinted windows, smiles of the missing.
Everything posted—bargain bids,
pleas for vital organs. No fourth wall
to drive out the elements: hail, fallout.
Today All Souls' Day.
Today when the souls go back.
Today the day of numbers, departures.
Where I wait inside another morning.
The saints, the statues left in the house
where a machine answers all voices.
The end has been delayed, it
missed a connection. No one can wait.
Bribery, blackmail—the heat keeps
leaves in place. I keep my place with the others,
I don't know how to drive them out.
The children are bundled, the heat in place.
Where we wait inside another morning,
we miss a connection.
Today the souls go back: bribery and blackmail
are no good. They forget our phone numbers.
They can't wait to be missing.
A machine keeps answering all voices.
The end is coming.
We are keeping our place.
We are forming a line.

The Arsonist's Letters Michael Tyrell

Delicatessen

(after Hurricane Sandy & 3 nights of no power)

In the delicatessen a last avocado.
Black, pulpy—a kind of soft grenade.

I set it down
for probably nobody.

I step out—not through doors
but through clear plastic tatters
shimmering in a doorframe.

Hothouse roses on the shelves outside;
hyacinths in foiled cups.

*

Calling storms by dumb names—
not the shabbiest way of neutering disaster,
I think.

      Like the pit bull called Cuddles,
the Lover's Lane near the sewage treatment plant—

Even *All Saints' Day*,
when you think about it.
Today, when I say, *I have it good*,
meaning, *better than others*,

& the children screaming *Help*
then *Made you look*, meaning
We tricked you—

*

The Arsonist's Letters Michael Tyrell

But hyacinths in November!
You should see them!

Hyacinths make roses ridiculous by contrast.

Just look at the roses
hyperventilating in their cellophane shawls—

Pluck their cat claws & they don't object…

I want to grab someone passing & ask
the riddle that flowers won't answer—
how much beauty
comes from never saying no?

*

Maybe someone *will* answer me.
That's why I keep my mouth shut.

*

But not the sour-mouthed cashier—
she handles the bills,
she carelessly dabs the lemon wedge
she keeps by the side of the register.

Never a word from her.
Maybe the balances chafe
the tongue as well as the fingers.

She doesn't need to keep an eye peeled—
the cameras do it all.

If I could teach one art, it
would be how to go home unanswered,
empty-handed—

*

But what about the sidewalk Cyclops,

the all-seeing tattoo on the bald guy's head,
who once, I swear, called me by my right name,

who saw me frowning in sunlight—

*That & this so bad, Tyrell, you ain't
seen the darkest yet…*

The subway's closed tonight—
what darkest dark can he guard now?

*

I think I'd grow to like it—

the terrible wisdom
of stillness. The stomach, unchurning,
hollow as a prop.

The circles moving around them,
the cashier & the Cyclops.
The flowers too, if they can
reckon up anything besides their own mutilation.

Maybe they can sense
the babies wheeling by at warp speed…
who seem too light, having
little to them, or too much—an eye,
a name, some inarticulate rage,
all that's needed to be called a storm.

*

*And what's a blackout, Tyrell?
Afraid of roaches?
Maybe you'll make some new friends.*

*

The Arsonist's Letters Michael Tyrell

And why hyacinths, why November?

Why rooted, not cut through, uncovered,
combining two colors?

Celestial blue, arterial purple,
maybe earth thinking both of heaven
& the blood in the sexes—

Thinking not only of a man-boy
turned into something beautifully inhuman
because a god looked at him once

but also picturing women
who know how to hide,

the woman in the jungle camp called
Hyacinth?

76, secreting herself
under a cot while the cult leader
in the pavilion makes nine hundred others
lie on the ground one last time,

& they won't rise again,

the cups on the ground like white flowers.

The toxins, red and purple in the cups,
around the roses of their mouths.

& Hyacinth who knows how to hide,
how to wait for the last to drink
even as the writer of the last note

summons those particulars
that are terrible for being so ordinary—

a gray sky, a dog barking,
a bird on a telephone wire.

White night, the leader calls it.

Stepping over the people on the ground—
Hyacinth & the moon
can rise in the white, humid night.

*

November then;
November now.

A kind of soft grenade
I set down for probably nobody.

Would I eat the goddamn flowers
if I thought they'd answer?

Made you look is all we can say

The Arsonist's Letters Michael Tyrell

Fayum

The Arsonist's Letters Michael Tyrell

All the Unreal Animals

Larries emerge in October, annuals
like mayflies that come out in June
or groundhogs afraid of their own shadows—

the running out of chlorophyll is a music they can hear
that draws them from their terminal
burrows, more than the fires licking over the wooden giraffes

that have the memories of elephants
when it comes to their early colors they wore,
and the Larries when they see this begin paradoxically

undressing like hypothermia victims,
off come the layers as from onions or garter snakes,
and under the hot moon they look for marriage,

their compound eyes a lightning-bug
code, lasers in the places where night
makes capsules where every Larry lies waiting,

convinced because all the other Larries look alike
he's being deceived—a world of reflective
tricks and rungless ladders—and only

in sleep, a dream being had before the relentless
color is turned back on, in the moment a human
snips an aberrant thread from the layers of hair

as though a tail grew on her head overnight,
the Larry's extinction alarm clock dies and mating's done,
love is the thing you and the Larry see almost once and never again,

and another human—I saw him on the train

The Arsonist's Letters Michael Tyrell

early tonight—twisted his wedding band like a cap
from a jug of acidy wine, to the tip of his finger

but not quite fully off he twisted the such-and-such karat knot
and because it was November when we got off the train
and I let the crowd take him from me, I knew

it was over again, the chance to ask
a species what does it call God, and in all the streets
not a Larry to be found.

Alice, Sweet Alice

(after the 1976 film, directed by Alfred Sole)

When the B-movie father enters an abandoned warehouse
he won't leave alive it's understood:
he's doing it to save his daughter. He has the dumb courage

of people in horror movies, and we somehow feel
for him—he's not going to the top out of morbid
curiosity. I don't recognize the actor's name

or face—the credits call this the actor's debut,
and this makes the character's fate surprisingly
poignant: he's doing it to prove his daughter's

not the killer, he's doing it to get her released
from the juvenile institution where she trashes
a polygraph machine and conceals her menstruation

from her mother. She likes translucent masks;
she likes to put on a hag mask under the translucent mask
to frighten her younger sister, the family favorite.

I have sisters I've never met, let alone
had the chance to torment, or be tormented by.
I've tried to locate them on the Net, but the names

get no hits, and they live in another country.
My father, declared dead by social security records,
is no help; or else he's all help, silent saint, Romeo the Silent,

so I turn to the movie where the cops
bumble their search; the assassinated president
in an oil-painting in the precinct emits frustration,

conspiracy. Below my apartment the warehouse

The Arsonist's Letters Michael Tyrell

on the market, and next to that the boulevard's eighteen-wheelers
scraping the concrete where night-shift factory workers

have just crossed halfway, to the divider—
also called an island, an island on the freeway.
Planters have jammed in their geraniums—

why, to make the euphemism more plausible?
The flowers memorialize no one. But their disintegration
and ascension, their momentary exposures,

get replayed winter and summer,
and because they can't move, they're the ones who fail.
Not the people crossing—their laughter

spirals up like people laughing in a dream,
where because an errand is not fate
it will keep them perfectly safe.

The Passwords

The day I stop wishing for his money—cut myself
From his unwritten will—rub out the rainy-day faces
From the piggybank riches that can only be mine—

Then I'll be alone with my body—my disinherited
Rust—my still-workable bones—I'll take it for walks—
it will be my animal—

Short walks—on a low-numbered city street—
Days before Halloween—when the body
Has to be kept on a short leash—it might run off—

And I'll worry maybe my father—being among the dead—
Will find me—*don't look* I'll say—not even in store windows—
Everything a bare mirror to be stumbled into—

Not even in the jewelry shop at dusk—velvet throats
Stripped of their bling—
What will I have then but passwords—

This one to shut down the account—
This one to read the messages—
This one to not beg favors—of the remembered ones—

Remembered I mean in a codicil—
The dressed-up, walking by-people—
All the others made by the one who made me—

The Arsonist's Letters Michael Tyrell

Letter Sent Back in Time to Mussolini's Italy

Cataldo Amorese (born June 4, 1927; died June 13, 2002)

Only for a quid pro quo
would the widow
give the boy some food—

The way she told me
you told her   the story:

Bari, Italy, 1942, you the boy
     going hungry like everyone else,
fifteen years old, Mussolini's Italy—

a boy who takes off his shoes
     first when he undresses;

the widow, her hair let down
     not to make her look young

but because the heat is slowly freezing her to death.

About that food—
     it wasn't a loaf of bread; that's too easy—

you say, more likely,
a rancid soup, "a core of cabbage,
the peel of a potato
     in innards of a chicken and the foam that forms on stock."[1]

And who doesn't want to fuck the war away?

---

*
1
http://www.academiabarilla.com/the-italian-food-academy/books-italian-cuisine/wartime-cuisine.aspx, Academia Barilla, "Wartime Cuisine"

The Arsonist's Letters Michael Tyrell

I have no pictures of C.A.…
          I don't know if he has a grave…

Maybe if I made a bargain,
maybe in this way we are alike—
          I make the bargains.

But he has no face.

In the underground stations to this day,
portraits painted everywhere,
and other people's limbs, on their phones,
painted like the faces of Coptic coffins, *fayum*.

The war fucked away,
the rest of us fucked over.

*

But he always spoke, you said,
admiringly about Benito and Clara.…
the old myth he made the trains run on time!
Betty you mad already.
Amore I with my dear father.
His documents thinner than onionskin,
our man of letters,
I can't entirely hate a man of so few words.

My mother agreed—
          that's why the letters got kept,
not the pictures.

Not a single picture!
Wouldn't allow herself—

Disappearance wasn't enough for her;
she wanted every fetish gone.

More a novelist than a revisionist historian—

only memory to work with.

Is it too late to become the arsonist,
who spares no letters?

*

First Date

November 3, 1968. "They only play Frank Sinatra," my father told my mother at Luna's Bar in
Greenpoint, Brooklyn. "Incidentally, I'm married."

Her nickname for him now?
Fuckface.

*

The bodies of *Il Duce* & his *putana*,
dangling like goods in the market—
in the newsreel now on YouTube
the heroes firing their rocks
making holes that shouldn't be there,
and the place-names, I shouldn't love them,
the Piezzale Loreto, the ESSO station.

The Arsonist's Letters Michael Tyrell

Wearable Ammunition

The Arsonist's Letters Michael Tyrell

Hemingway

In Genoa, city where the *Mary Celeste*
    never arrives every day,
the hour to become a ghost isn't necessarily noon—

it's when the young American student named Hemingway
    reads, in the plaza,

The Collected Stories of her namesake—

reads the story of the white elephant hills again,

the story of the bickering lovers who say, *Please, please, please,*

if only they can keep the child out of their words
    it will never be born,

the hills along the Ebro
like skin through a fire-screen of trees.

*

Our itinerary claims
a stop   a stop   a return—

it's the vessels we have to trust,
the vessels always blameless,

like the Mary Celeste, amber alcohol
lozenges cached below deck,

its investigators whose verdict said
mutiny, fever ship—

The Arsonist's Letters Michael Tyrell

*

Please, please, please, we've said to each other,
        please: stop the tiff,
prolong the delirious thrust,

your carry-on you forgot at the Nice railway
        must be in Firenze now.

Somewhere on the train here,
the languages changed and the ocean changed its sex.

I think you want me to be
a character from another story,
someone who goes missing
and can be suitably mourned,

but the hills in Genoa look too
        green to be elephants—

it's like Papa's writing this
in the wrong universe,

        no child to argue about,

and the future, as always, a ghost ship,

we can board it only
when we've shed some mutinous skins,
La mer becoming *il mare*

Wormhole

So far it's like any reality,
scanty foreshadowing,
infestations of coincidence.
The Magi enter in sidewalk murals,
seldom in the flesh, on sidewalk.
Waiting not the story the map tells.
If the bus is symbolic
it is not clear where we are in the plot,
whether the action is rising
or we've swerved into a subplot.
I don't see any face I can't fathom
not meeting in some waiting room or other.
There's a lottery here like anywhere,
we must scratch and scratch
to make our nails metallic-black.
And rules about doubles abound
should we encounter them; there are
ropes to know. Who knows, we might
turn out to be the ghosts in this story,
though the budget won't accommodate
sci-fi monsters to wolf the city down.
Inconsequential light, through dirty windows,
touches the faces of the riders facing West.
Only one glances up, baffled and attentive,
like one reading Plato for the first time—
nothing not shadow,
and she can't stomach another illusion.
—*December 2016*

The Arsonist's Letters Michael Tyrell

Lontano

I live in buildings I never leave.
Someone's chopped up the lifeboats with an axe
though we're not at sea.
The heat makes the outside.
Something in water here
makes my hair fall out.
If there's a frame a face must come to fill it,
isn't that so? I wish that out my window
I could see a body of water
and a body washing up,
still human and alive.
I tried cutting out newspaper letters,
but now I'm my own hostage.
And two in love with me already.
My suitors know about each other.
Once there was a dance
and the three of us looked at two thrones,
all metallic and shining like tinfoil.
Late nights, we dial the rooms
where love's being made.
Our students get luckier than we do.
I hate them. They like me fine—
it's easy to love a bald doll.
I won't marry. I will marry.
I'll marry a student who collects dolls.
Mother writes to remind me
of my surgery.
Never forgave me, for
breaking open her body when
I fell out into the world.
She wants me in the
hands of others now.
One morning I go to the room with the papery table

The Arsonist's Letters Michael Tyrell

where I lie down
and the laser opens the hatch between my lids.
I'll be clear now, everyone will get me.
The suitors run off with each other.
I can smell my eye burning.

Murder in Sea Gate

Where there are woods, green
foliage now turns blonde. The telescoping

corridor in the Hall of Justice
is yellower & mustier than those leaves,

and the unlooked-for trails to jury duty
this time lead not to an exit door

but only deeper into the leaden courthouse,
where you're picked as an alternate

to hear the details of a murder in Sea Gate,
rule if the Russian girl at the bottom of the stairs

died at the hands of a vagrant
or her husband. The material witnesses

blame America—she was illegal
and couldn't seek help, even after

he chased her once, with a can of Raid in his hand,
through the Cyrillic cul-de-sacs of the gated community.

The real jurors nod off; the evidence photos
barely get winced at. Exhibit A is the ligature,

a coaxial, & you think you won't be able to tie on a scarf
for months, even when the single digits come; you won't even watch TV.

But the next morning, barely first frost, you drop
those vows, you flip to the weather channel & warm your throat with wool,

The Arsonist's Letters Michael Tyrell

walking into court you can almost forget that murderers
are usually those we know, the weapons our own utilities,

and the woods you've scribbled on a loose-leaf page
seem nowhere in particular—scraggly trees, no life in them, not even a
birdlike V.

The minute recess comes you swear
the drawing will join all the other wastebasket mistakes,

but still you wish you had color first to make a convincing failure,
something to show how foliage goes, just like that, from green to blonde.

Wound Care

Not even the dresser-top saints can see
how you unbutton your shirt tonight
to show me the ghost of a zipper
the sawbones left, taking back
their staples. All your summer
the taking out, sherd by sherd,
a kind of dig, the slug he left you with,
the rent-a-cop gunning for his baby mama,
who caught you by mistake.
Pizza-parlor aprons they dropped
over you, all the tattoos coming
up roses that night, and then
your other blood, their luggage, the
forgiveness from those who once said
we don't own you, you are dissed, you are not owned,
who didn't say the wounded
somehow are easiest reclaimed,
the saints they brought you
collapsed into wooden dolls,
who can't see, having been turned
to face the wall above the bed—
and like another kind of sniper
I'm above you lying down,
all our wearable ammunition unloaded
if not glittering still warm
when you say scar gonna fade quicker,
when you say shoot here.

The Arsonist's Letters Michael Tyrell

The Ones with Children

The Arsonist's Letters Michael Tyrell

Letter at the Security Gate

No harm you mean.
Only stowaways, your furies.

Their stone-turning dirty looks
only metaphor.

Your bone suit,
Turin relic, all veil.

Their names just the word
revenge in the dead language.

Easily hidden,
duty free. Minor grudges,

canceled apologies,
ordinary venom, no workers,

no brood cells,
skybridge, the bird, a sun in honey.

Empty pocket,
you lift your arms like an

angel in snow that isn't there.
The furies bite their tongues.

Their explosions only fiction.
Mostly. Removes smiles and rings

so Security lets you through
like brutal angels, a shoeless limbo.

The Arsonist's Letters Michael Tyrell

Worse, your suitcase the usual shadow,
your myth only a statistic.

From earth to earth, gate to terminal,
good girls, you carry them.

They love movies, having seen
them all, made them. Your movie.

Except they won't ever spoil the ending,
though you ask and ask, and you don't mind spoilers.

In Clinton Hill, After Seeing the House Where the Famous Poet Lived Until the Area Became "Unsafe"

Swastikas on a trashcan. The poet
        moved when the area became unsafe.
History gentrifies. The realtors rename
        the streets, terraces and heights and palisades
pulled from the ass of thesaurus.
        This plaque tells you who
lived in this brownstone
        was generous or good, died for a good
cause. Obsolete geography
        gets a child's globe left
by the street garbage,
        and the seashell, cracked in half,
no longer supports a hoax
        of an ocean recorded inside.
You are heading to a park
        where you find the explorer's likeness;
his discovery earned him a statue.
        The donors' plated names on the benches
gleam in the sun, bribing, imploring
        to be remembered, and you,
also known as I, also known as we,
        don't remember
when the world decided it could live without you,
        or why the I's eye
is so small, a cold-hearted martinet,
        a cutter and paster of mismatched letters
like the author of a ransom
        note. It clips what is not unpleasant—
the fountain—then puts it next
        to the passing face of the burned woman.
It could turn away as quick
        as the blind ignorantly walk over the dead,
also known as *them*.

The Arsonist's Letters Michael Tyrell

        The dead are the only ones in absolute possession
of their pronoun.
        What does the *I* want?
What was taken from it—novelty.
        When was it taken?
Sometime in childhood—
        childhood, that obstacle,
like a protestor blocking the parade's advance,
        until suddenly moving
becomes more important than winning,
        and then because the *I* has agreed
to stop crying it is given
        a bright balloon to hold,
or its helium holds the *I* up,
        novelty stretched and bruised as the
impatiens in the windowbox—
        those ringed boxers
surrounded and bet against,
        chained and writhing.

In Winter the Only Green

1   No children for me
except in stories, sister
& brother lost in the forest,
never aging of course, & no forest
near my flat, only hollyhocks
& sick Dutch elms, an eyesore
shack, a crippled blunt thing,
burnt like the woman
the children hurled into a kiln
to get free.

2   They're never free,
the ones with children.
They never sleep,
but must scare
the children to keep them
home, a made-up
forest that every year
seems more fiction
than the hag
in the eyesore shack.
It's a mirage;
hunger makes it
look like sugar.

3   If I can't be tracked
on the machines,
I don't exist.
Near landing, the flight
circling the lit-up map
we live on now.

The Arsonist's Letters Michael Tyrell

    How dainty
    the city's circuitry,
    the plane also—
    like an egg
    handled by children
    pretending they have children.

4   Children,
    I write to you
    from the city
    where in winter
    the only green's
    the go signal reflected
    on storm windows.
    The mothers and fathers
    bring you, girl & boy,
    neighbors in the alphabet,
    to life for their
    young insomniacs,
    & your stepmother's husband
    who promises
    he'll collect you,
    tells you you're
    too big to believe
    in witches, spares
    them a story about fate—
    how, with crumbs, without,
    collected or otherwise,
    we come to harm.

At Salvation

        You mustn't blame us at the register
who hold your bills to buzzing light
       so the blood threads
can verify tender or what-not.
       Everyone's a thief in here, though
thanks for paying cash for the alien family
       in the scalloped picture. Better pray
you become like them, the happy people
       who don't make
history but slip, as into B-movie
       quicksand or something
more comfortable. Must avoid
       especially your own gaze, foxhole where
you might have to choose a god,
       cling to the now like sacred transactions,
two dimes for change, childless
       twin couple, moon faces moon-cool
to the touch. You don't work at Salvation
       where at least the door
says thank you come back,
       paper clock hands point to everyone must go.
We're sorry business sucks today,
       every sucker home remembering a war or two,
but what were you doing all afternoon,
       browsing our aisles?
What are you—army of one?
       Among the ramrod mannequins
drill commanders—
       you got your family, your
snapshot lifted from the buck bin.
       Thanks to some
obscenity of light and paper everyone
       still rings gleeful around their

The Arsonist's Letters Michael Tyrell

firepit. So what if you can't tell which
        animal; it's a charred flower
and history has had its office hours.
        So don't let the door hit
you in the ass, which would be
        sidewalked if we caught
you using us in this poem. Go now.
        The graffiti gate, screeching low,
cuts even daylight to its raw knees.

Marathon

Tomorrow we'll lose an hour of light. Tomorrow the living will run the trained horses of their bodies almost to death. I can picture them now, even though I'm in yesterday's news, the digitized necropolis; when a name comes up a handful in ten thousand it's like the pale forearm of someone drowning: an almost erotic rescue. Then uncertainty again. A hundred years ago, to be gassed in the forest, then a Paris hospital. Untraceable for eighteen months. Was there something besides the wounding that kept him? I've spent my life envying the fugitives, but he came home, climbed ladders with one leg, the houses of Kent Street got painted, and he fathered someone who brought me here. The ladders have to be moved, everything has to be put aside for the runners; bless those who brought in the green bronze hay-bales, like something from the intractable past, to divide the watchers from the watched; liminal fodder, bundled light.

The Arsonist's Letters Michael Tyrell

Documentary for Eleanor M., Who Was Mistaken for the Kidnapped Lindbergh Baby in March, 1932

It would have to be reenactment disguised as newsreel

WINTHROP PARK, SEVENTEENTH WARD, BROOKLYN

shot of the lawn filmed in black and white
and gunmetal benches close-up on the first cop's
mutton-chop face after the title card fades
his cockeyed twitch that seems to say *I know this scene's absurd*
a pram pulled over by the cops like some bank robber's getaway car and
medium shot of your reenactment
mother
in cloche hat and spring coat too shocked to argue
(have they made baby walking a crime?)
conflicting accounts your mother policestationed
for her questioning for your own good
and you given to the doctor and then they hand you back
OR it's fast simple the second cop sees the wrong sex
under the pins of your cloth diaper
and he almost drops you handing back

*

That handing back—again and again, even if you can't possible remember,
you know they might have kept you,
filed you with the other
mistaken identities and counterfeit dollars all the wrong wrongfully kept

as if to have an alibi
in case the actual never materializes

*

It would have to include

The Arsonist's Letters Michael Tyrell

a montage of other baby carriages

getting pulled over all across America

Lindbergh Lindbergh every infant in America changeling

mandrake Lindbergh

*

Interview excerpts:
I too am one of history's deleted scenes, but I remember it
do you?

Sound is only recently invented and no talkie can convey the moment—not the last— the
world insisting This is
Mine, no match, but what you are will do just as well.

*

Eleanor, silvery cousin, blind acquaintance—

I don't know who gets taken
who returned safe,
why even the globe stunt-flying
doesn't shield others.
The baby I've chosen
to play you in the documentary
will not stop crying,
which by all accounts
you did not do even then.

Two Postcards

1 In a Station of the MTA

> The cradle rocks above an abyss, and common sense tells us that our
> existence is but a brief crack of light
> between two eternities of darkness.
> —Nabokov, *Speak, Memory*

The woman on the subway platform this morning,
clutching sonogram snapshots
of her not-yet-born—
she didn't flinch as one image
fluttered to the tracks,
she didn't notice or care, she was running somewhere—
the image was not blown away
as you or I wanted it to be blown away,
and the woman made her transfer,
trimesters still ahead of her.
We didn't make the closing doors
and didn't want to look down at the tracks,
so we checked out the defaced ads—
life can be as ~~inspiring~~ USELESS as your dreams.
No one dies a virgin. Death fucks you in the end.
A response: Don't sound 2 bad 2 me.
The clock: no pointers, a cable's dangling
black tongue, maybe a souvenir
from one of the dark eternities. Already
we feel the concrete trembling,
as if Nabokov is right, we stand up,
wide-eyed in our cradle trembling together--

2 McCarren Park (Known as Needle Park in the Seventies and Eighties)

(Russian Postcards For Sale, Never Sent--sign in Greenpoint, Brooklyn shop.)

If you lived in Norilsk you'd be home by now,
but most likely you'd just be dead.

The Arsonist's Letters Michael Tyrell

Norilsk, northernmost city in the world, with its short human
life expectancy and nickel pollution that make all trees catch fire
wherever they're brought, won't have trees or you. Your

born-into parcel of the Earth tilts willfully toward the sun,
so you have spring, the doll in the dugout's
mud, Chernobyl baby, winter's artifact sprouting moss like whiskers....

It almost makes you stop wondering if you left the gas on,
the door unlocked. So this is spring:
to be the dogwood's bitch;
the other place incinerating, surely;
the children closer, who want to stay in the park playing war...

You carry an unsent card in your coat like immunity papers
from one ruined place to another
where it is, at least, somehow,
always spring.

To Have Them

Even my beloved bees set upon me today when I numbly knocked aside their sugar feeder, and I am all over stings....—Sylvia Plath, in a letter to her mother, October 1962

One week into lockdown
the dogwoods flowering
look more foam than flower.

Flowers at the ground and in branches
a white at the lips like a first symptom.

A stillness, as in post-seizure.

Maybe a first symptom, noticing.
Like losing smell, shedding the taste buds, the tongue's

scant flowers. How many of us
flowering now insignificantly, not noticeably?

Faces in boxes on the phone
and faces beaming through screens in Lombardy.

And still it's spring like the sum of many previous
springs. The outside what you remember,

not the hours at home.
The beloved bees you can't see in the rain.
All along building and dismantling the flowers.

The sirens and the mourning doves
like the mask and the rubber gloves.

Like the sum of springs, like noticing.

The Arsonist's Letters Michael Tyrell

Like, *I am all over stings.*

I go outside.
I put each of them on.

Against all sense
wanting skin against skin again.
More than the words and the masks
and the gloves.
For someone in the world,
to topple me, take them off me—
to have to touch me, talk to me
to have them.

Apology to the Letters

Because P. was pulled through the river,
because R. ordered a special oven online
to finish it all like an elaborate recipe,
and S. didn't go how we expected—
mid-tirade—
but no, lingered, radiated,
shorn, for years, still writing…

Letters, forgive me,
like someone afraid of J's planchette
I can't spell you out to certification.
Maybe because I've lived too long among

the Dutch alphabet roads,
because the delinquent padlocks shine
at the end of the jetty
clasping nothing but their own knots,

because I must walk the dog
and carry you, my initials,
like Scrabble tiles
in a jacket pocket, because
to change them into runes,
I must believe light moves with purpose
even through grids,
because Manhattanhenge,

because the sinner in me
still wrestles daily with the city druid,
because it's the words, not the
rivers, not the cancers, that are killing me,
though I can curl up in some,
like *drooth* that means a dry place,

The Arsonist's Letters Michael Tyrell

like the character we'd write
for human if we could see ourselves
from the outside-in,
something like tooth and drool,
form and hunger
in nothing but the present tense.

The Arsonist's Letters Michael Tyrell

Notes

Birthday Anniversary Sympathy Blank
Abigail Folger, murdered by members of the Manson Family in August, 1969, is the "coffee heiress" referred to near the end of the poem. Decades after her death, she was still on at least one retailer's mailing list.

Alphabet City, 1994
The "*trompe-l'oeil*" refers to reversible figures, ambiguous pictures that, according to the viewer's perception, can be "read" in more than one way.

According to legend, heiress Sarah Lockwood Winchester famously ordered the construction of 160 rooms in her San Jose, California, mansion to fool the ghosts of those killed by her family's guns.

Bottle Episode
Heisenberg (aka Walter White) and Pinkman are characters from the TV series *Breaking Bad*.

Letters Written Near the End of the Cold War
The poem derives some of its narrative context from events recounted in Debbie Nathan's book *Sybil Exposed*: a moment in early 1990s America when the diagnosis of multiple personality disorder skyrocketed and cases of "Satanic panic" proliferated.

Delicatessen
Hyacinth Thrash was the single survivor discovered in the wake of the Peoples Temple mass murder-suicide in Jonestown, Guyana, in November, 1978.

Some late lines in the poem paraphrase a letter found at the site.

Alice, Sweet Alice
The poem uses details and images from Alfred Sole's 1976 movie *Alice, Sweet Alice*, released at various times under that title and also under *Communion* and

The Arsonist's Letters Michael Tyrell

Holy Terror.

The Passwords
When Helen Klein Ross solicited poems for her anthology *The Traveler's Vade Mecum* (giving each of us a template phrase drawn from A.C. Baldwin's original 1853 *Traveler's Vade Mecum*, or *Instantaneous Letter Writer*) the one she sent me was "The Heirs Will Not Consent."

Letter Sent Back in Time to Mussolini's Italy
"[A] *core of cabbage...*" is quoted from the Academia Barilla "*Wartime Cuisine.*" webpage at http://www.academiabarilla.com/the-italian-food-academy/books-italian-cuisine/wartime-cuisine.aspx.

Hemingway
Fragments of Ernest Hemingway's "*Hills Like White Elephants*" appear.

Lontano
"Lontano" in Italian means "far away."

In Clinton Hill, After Seeing the House Where the Famous Poet Lived Until the Area Became "Unsafe"
Notes in *A Marianne Moore Reader* inspired the poem's title.

Apology to the Letters
Thanks to Jannie Dresser, whose prompt to write a poem using some Scots' English (in this case, the word *drooth*), was instrumental.

Acknowledgements

My profound thanks to the many friends and colleagues who encouraged me through the progression of these poems over many years. I'm also grateful to the editors of the following magazines and anthologies, where some of this work originally appeared in earlier forms:

The Bellevue Literary Review: Intruder
The Best American Poetry: Delicatessen
Dunes Review: Apology to the Letters
Fogged Clarity: The Garden, Letters Written Near the End of the Cold War, Nixon, The Passwords
la fovea: Alice, Sweet Alice
Gulf Coast: Birthday Anniversary Sympathy Blank
HIV Here and Now: Birthday Anniversary Sympathy Blank
The Iowa Review: Delicatessen
Margie: The American Journal of Poetry: In Clinton Hill, Where the Famous Poet Lived Until the Area Became Unsafe
Mudlark: In a Station of the MTA, Murder in Sea Gate
The Night Heron Barks: Bottle Episode, Marathon
The Paris Review: Transit
Ploughshares: Alphabet City, 1994
La Presa: Letter at the Security Gate; Russian Postcards for Sale, Never Sent
Rasputin: A Poetry Thread: Documentary for Eleanor Marzano
Documentary for Eleanor M., Who Was Mistaken for the Kidnapped Lindbergh Baby in March, 1932
Sycamore Review: Landscape with a Burning City; The Primal Scene
The Traveler's Vade Mecum: The Passwords
What Rough Beast: To Have Them; Wormhole

The Arsonist's Letters Michael Tyrell

A Note about The Author

Michael Tyrell is the author of *The Wanted* (National Poetry Review, 2012) and *Phantom Laundry* (Backlash, 2017) and, with Julia Spicher Kasdorf, edited *Broken Land: Poems of Brooklyn* (NYU Press, 2007). His poems have appeared in *Agni*, *The Best American Poetry*, *The Iowa Review*, *The Paris Review*, *Ploughshares*, *The Yale Review*, and many other publications. A native of Brooklyn, he teaches at New York University.

The Arsonist's Letters Michael Tyrell

www.ingramcontent.com/pod-product-compliance
Lightning Source LLC
Chambersburg PA
CBHW021146060526
44107CB00146B/1328/J